BURNING BLUES GUITAR

BY KIRK FLETCHER

To access video visit:
www.halleonard.com/mylibrary

Enter Code
2913-6804-2941-5347

ISBN 978-1-4950-1672-1

HAL•LEONARD®
CORPORATION
7777 W. BLUEMOUND RD. P.O. BOX 13819 MILWAUKEE, WI 53213

In Australia Contact:
Hal Leonard Australia Pty. Ltd.
4 Lentara Court
Cheltenham, Victoria, 3192 Australia
Email: ausadmin@halleonard.com.au

Visit Hal Leonard Online at
www.halleonard.com

CONTENTS

INTRODUCTION

Burning Blues Guitar represents some of my basic roadmaps to get you out playing with other people, because that's when the magic happens. A lot of folks think blues is simple, and in a way, it is. But therein lies the beauty.

There are many ways to approach any given blues song, and in this book/video, we will dig into some of those. We will get into various rhythm ideas—everything from backing up a harmonica player to Texas-style rock and roll, different approaches to shuffles, and slow blues. Also, we will get into some lead playing—working on how to build a solo and create phrasing ideas all over the fretboard.

I hope you will enjoy this lesson as much as I did doing it. So grab your guitar and let's start digging into some blues!

All the best,
Kirk Fletcher

About the Video

The accompanying videos can be accessed for download or streaming by visiting **www.halleonard.com/mylibrary** and entering the code found on page 1. The rhythm tab notation in this book matches the sequence of the performances and lessons in the videos, so you can follow along and use for practice.

Kirk Fletcher – Burning Bluesman

Widely considered one of the best blues guitarists in the world, Kirk Fletcher has commanded the respect and acclaim of critics, peers, and fans across the globe. He is a four-time Blues Music Award nominee and has played with a variety of popular artists, including a four-year role as lead guitarist of the Fabulous Thunderbirds. He is also the frontman of his own band, having released three studio albums and a live album. A fourth studio album is currently in the works.

RHYTHM GUITAR

Introduction

Shuffle

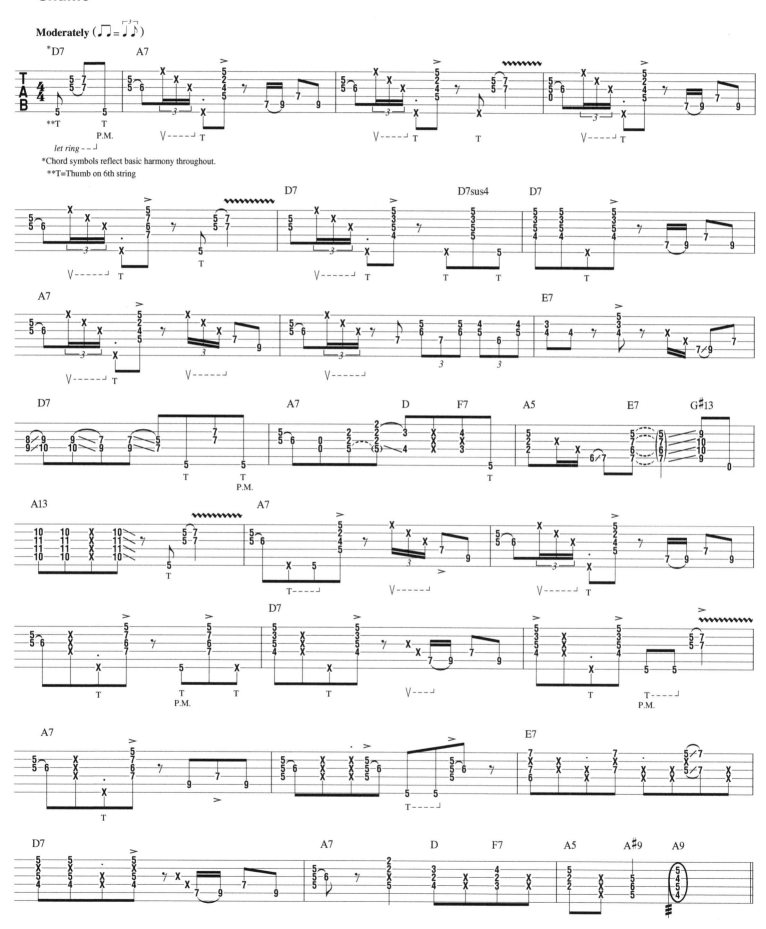

*Chord symbols reflect basic harmony throughout.

**T=Thumb on 6th string

Texas Blues

Grinder

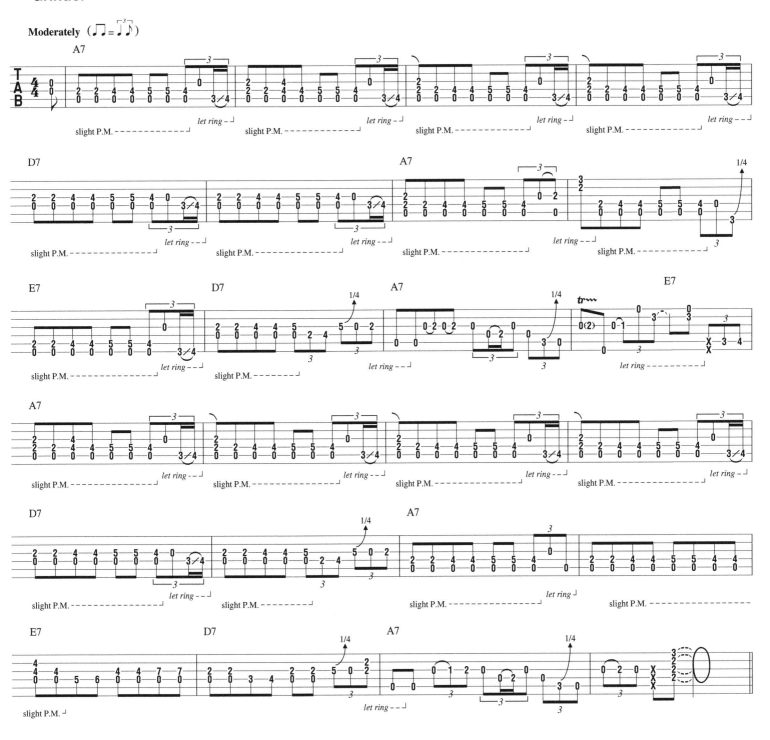

Grinder Basics

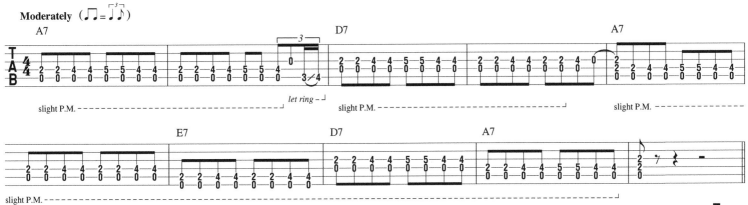

Grinder Variation

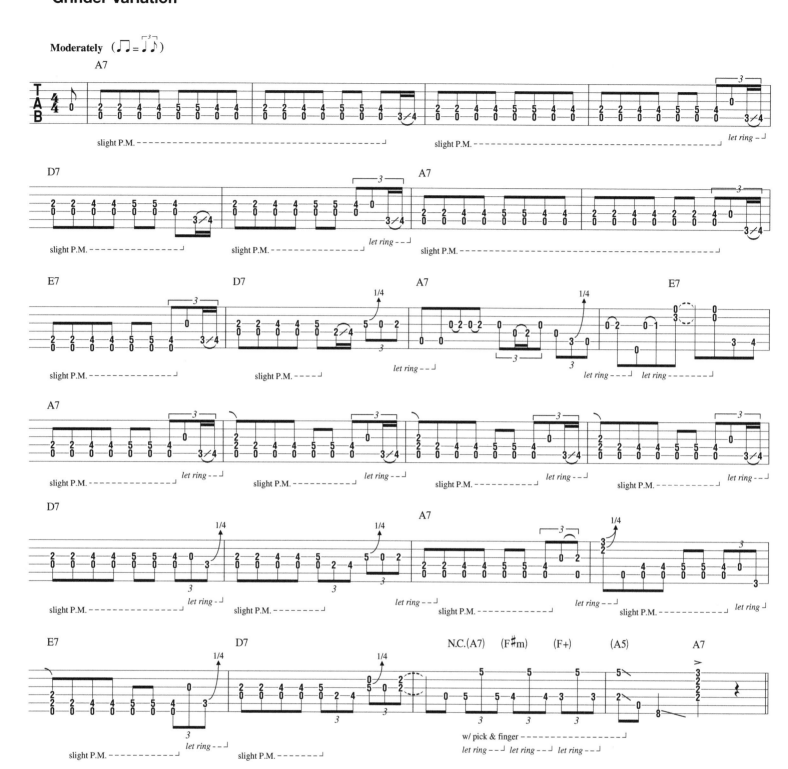

Straight 8th Rock and Roll

Rock and Roll

Rock and Roll RH

Moderately fast

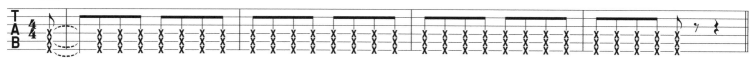

Rock and Roll RH with accents

Moderately fast

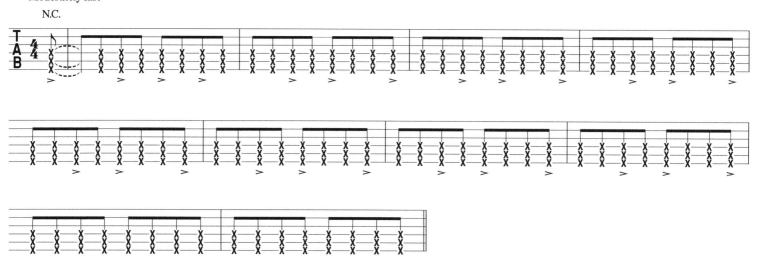

Rock and Roll LH

Moderately fast

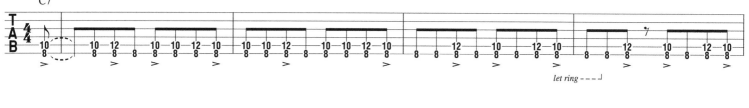

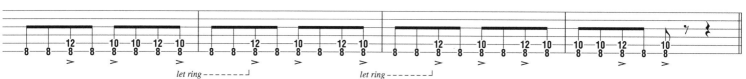

Rock and Roll All Together

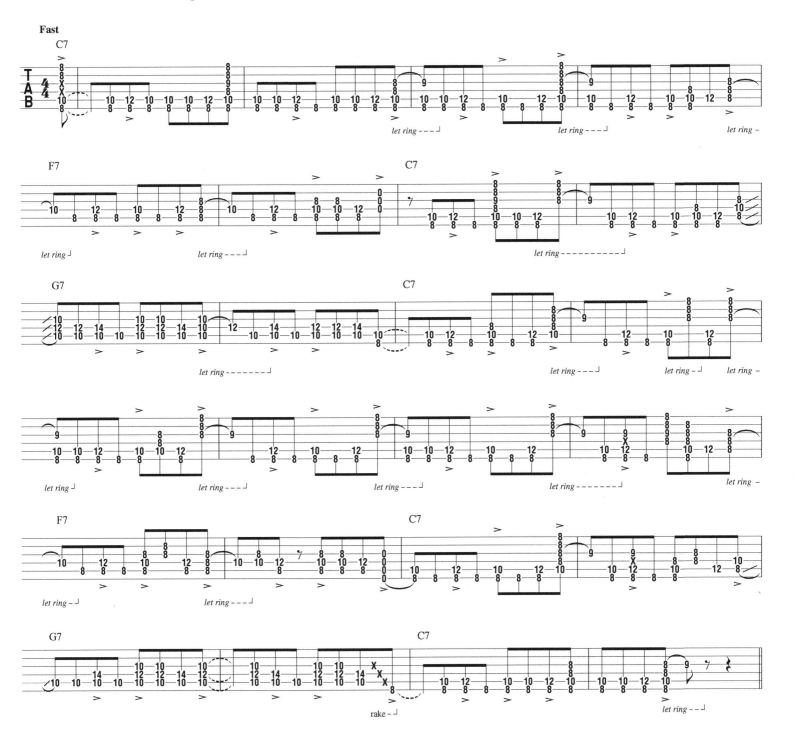

Chicago Blues

Sonny Boy

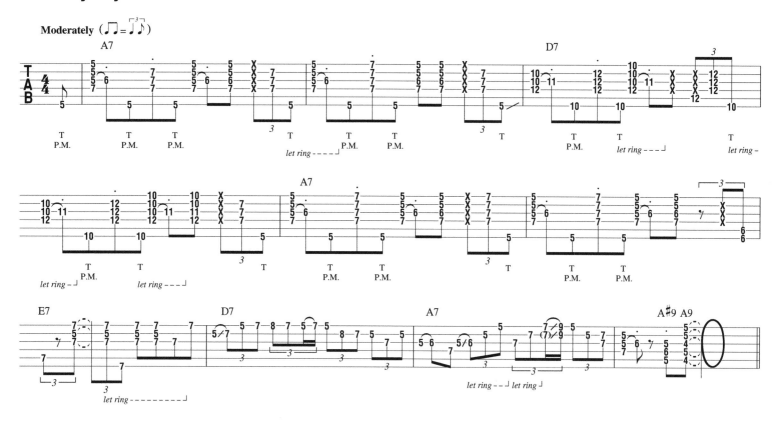

Jimmy Rogers

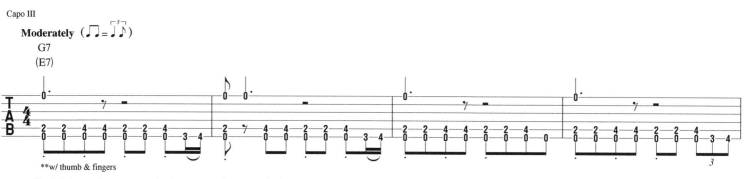

*Symbols in parentheses represent chord names respective to capoed guitar.
Symbols above represent actual sounding chords. Capoed fret is "0" in tab.

**Sound downstemmed notes with thumb; upstemmed notes w/ fingers.

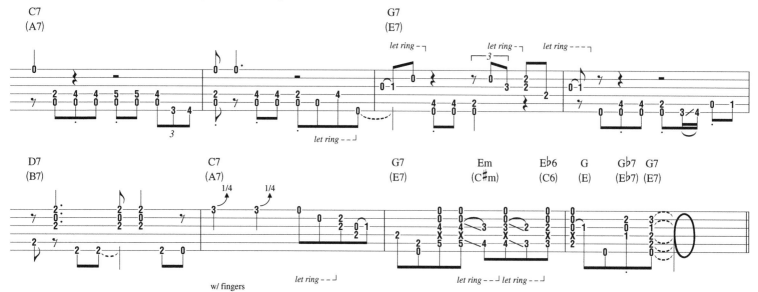

Jimmy Rogers Basics 1

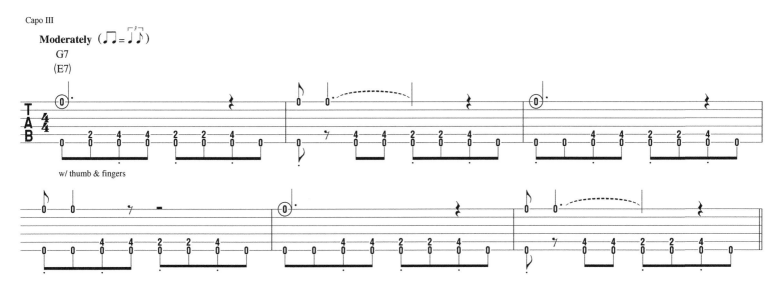

w/ thumb & fingers

Jimmy Rogers Basics 2

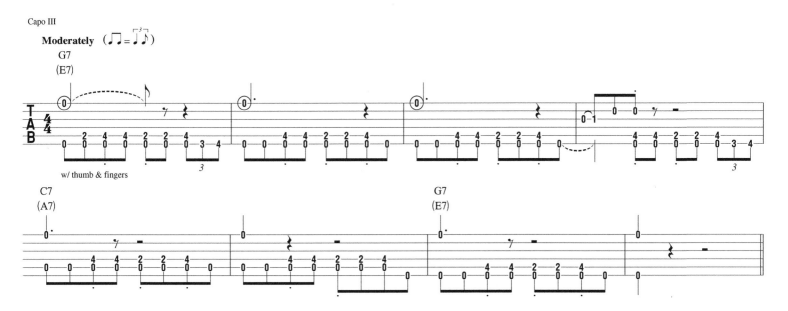

w/ thumb & fingers

Jimmy Rogers Turnaround

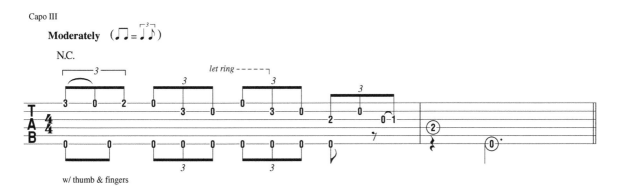

w/ thumb & fingers

Jimmy Rogers Walk-Down

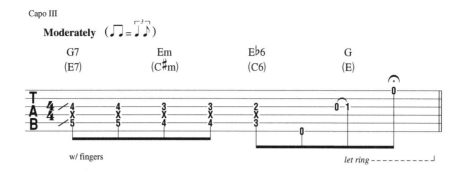

Jimmy Rogers All Together

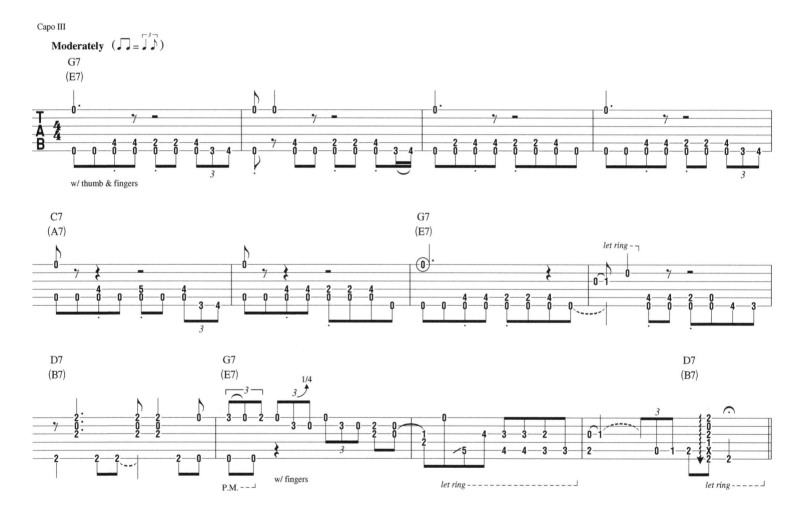

Sonny Boy Rhythm

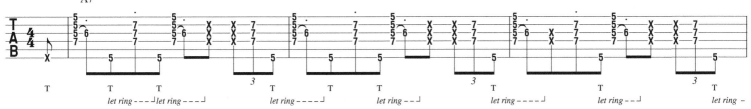

Sonny Boy RH

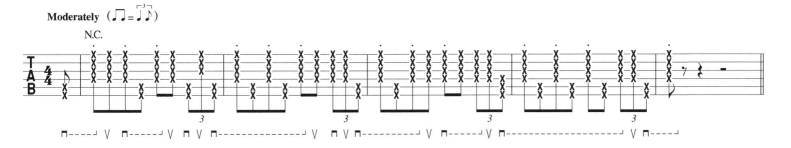

Sonny Boy slow

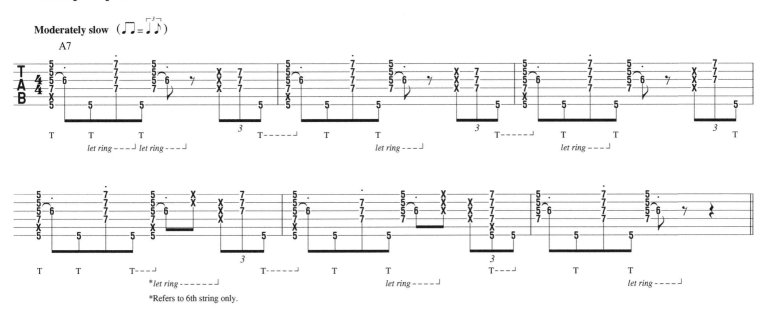

*Refers to 6th string only.

Sonny Boy Turnaround

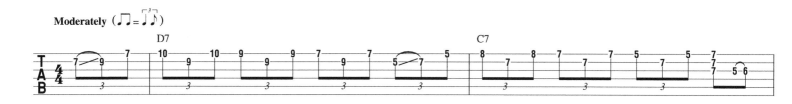

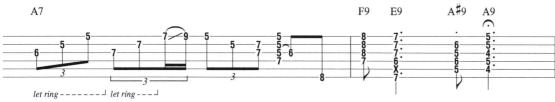

Sonny Boy Turnaround slow

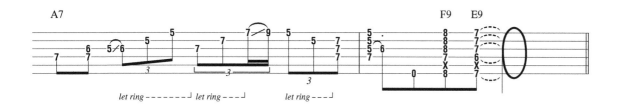

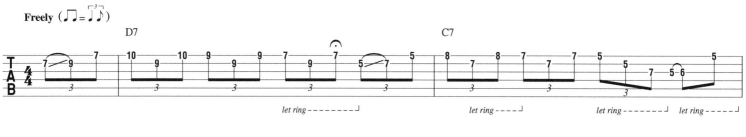

Sonny Boy All Together

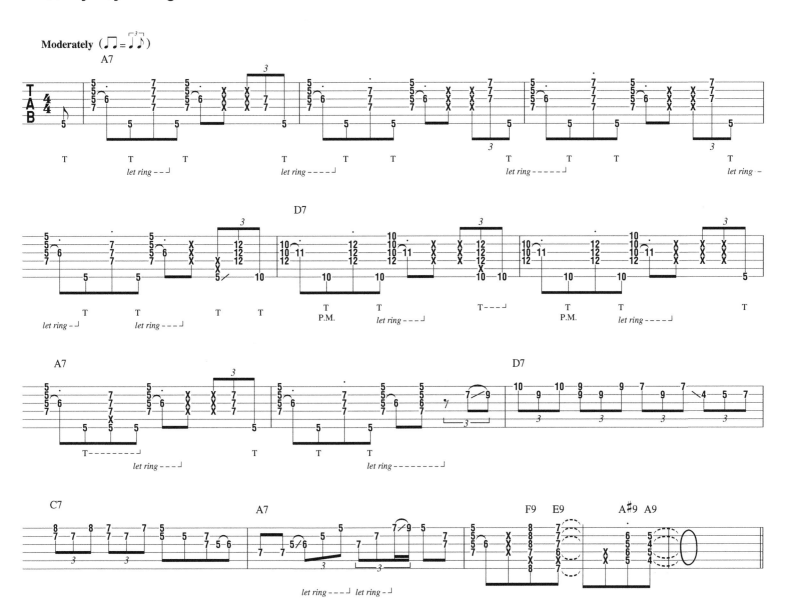

West Coast Jump

Jump Blues

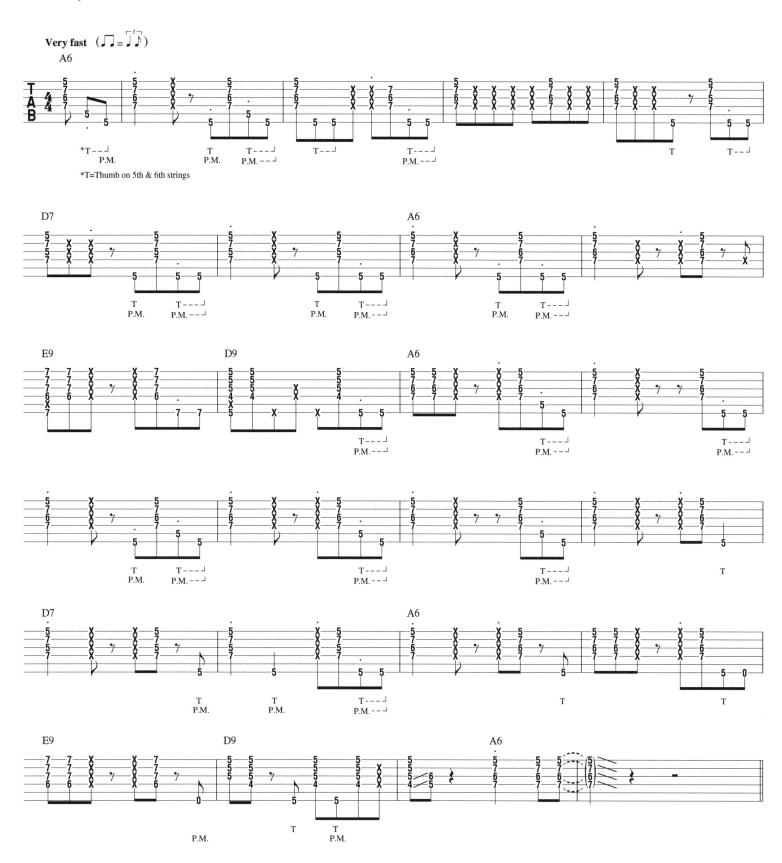

Jump Blues RH

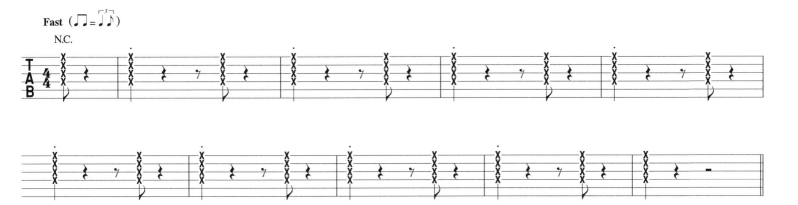

Jump Blues LH

Jump Blues All Together

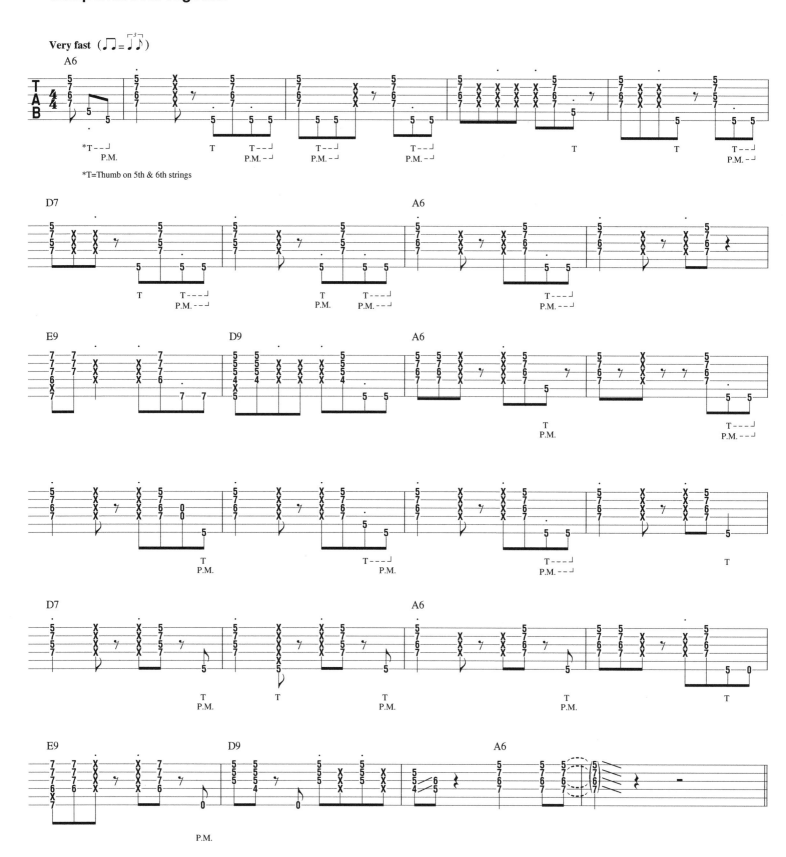

Funky Blues

Funky Blues

Moderately

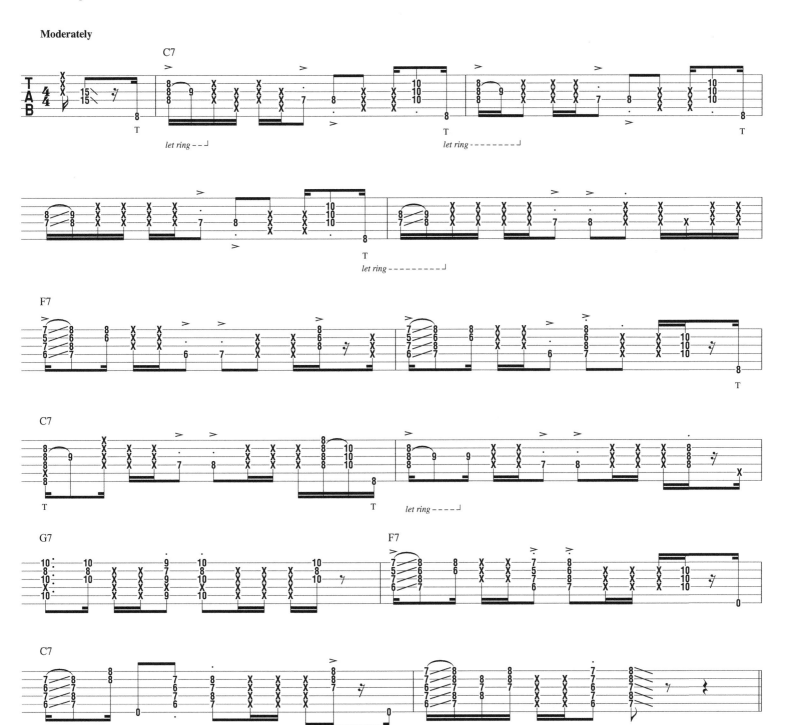

Funky Blues RH

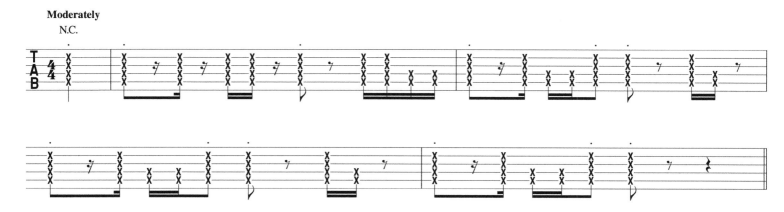

Funky Blues LH

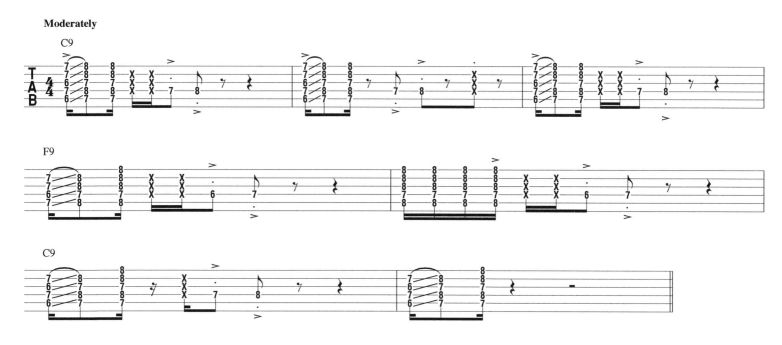

Funky Blues Chords

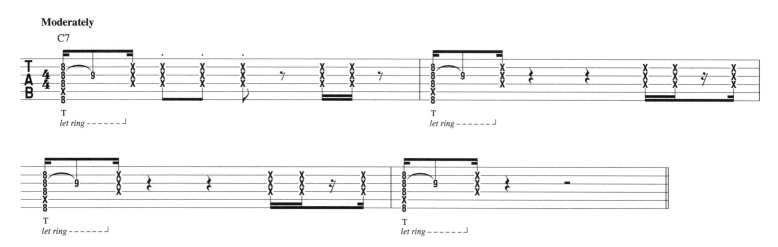

Funky Blues Single Notes

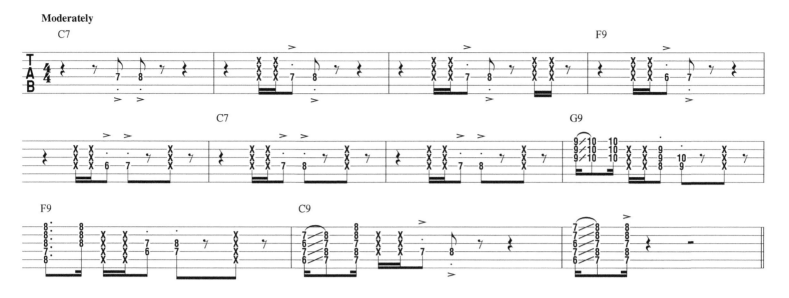

Funky Blues All Together

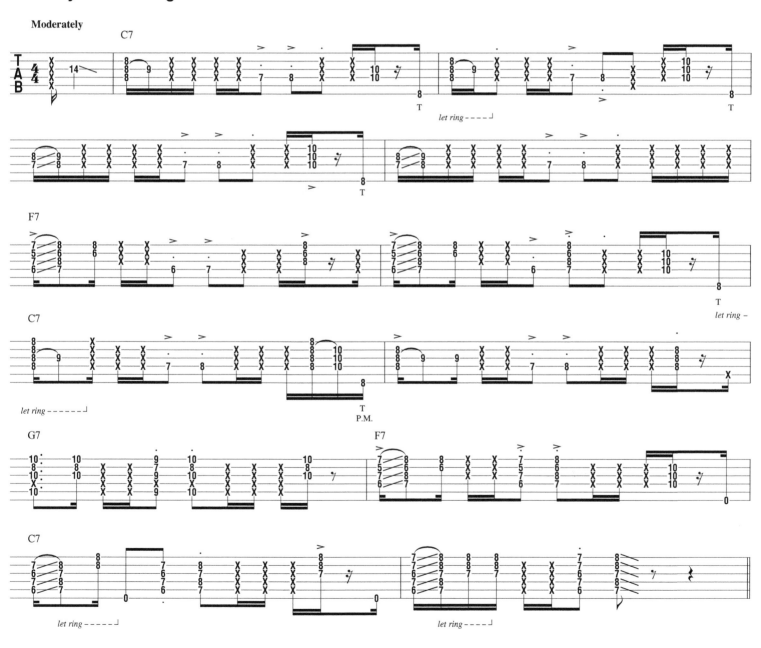

Slow Blues

Slow Blues

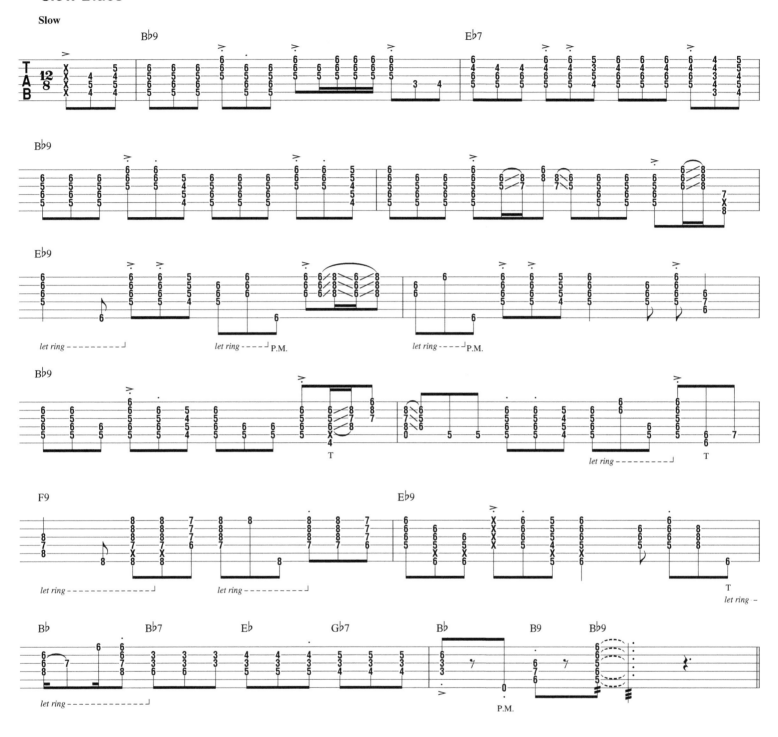

Slow Blues RH

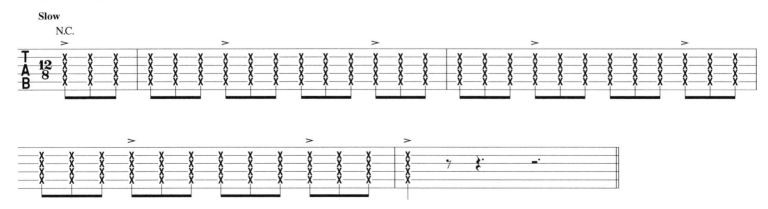

Slow Blues LH

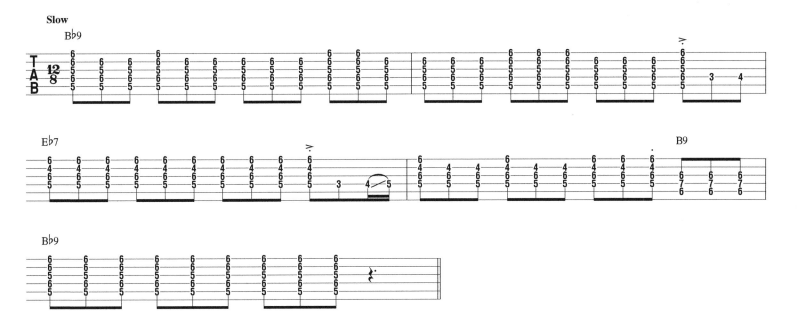

Slow Blues LH w/ slides

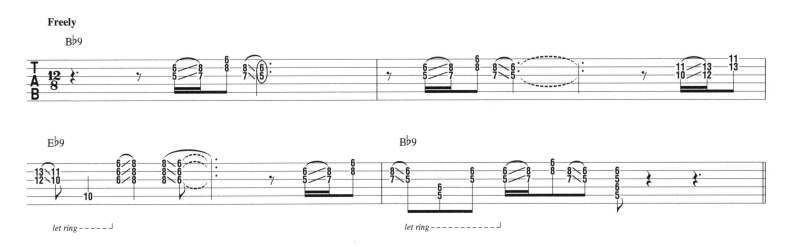

Slow Blues All Together

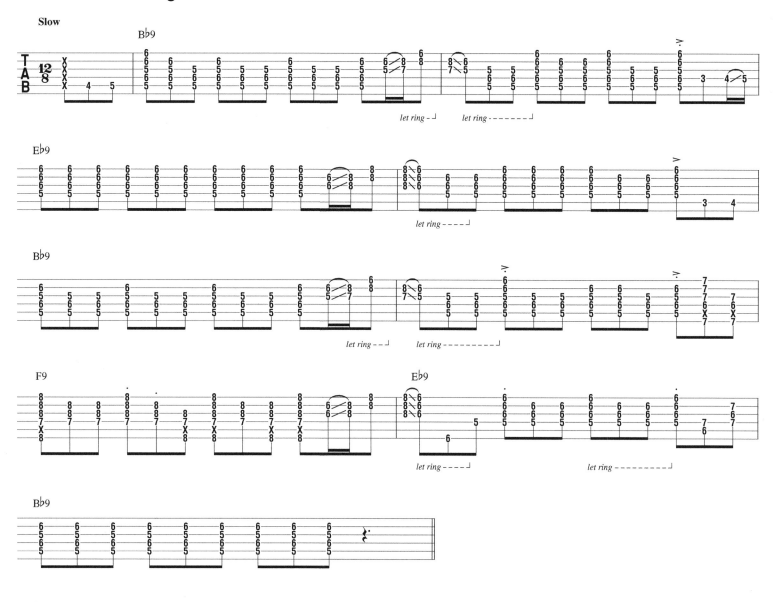

Standard Slow Blues

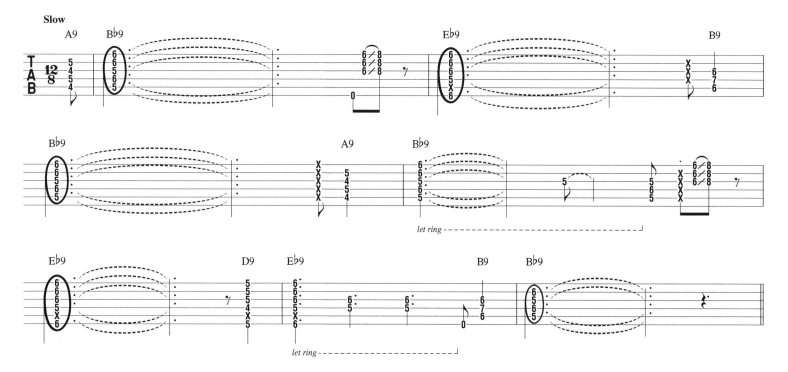

Kirk's Slow Blues

Slow

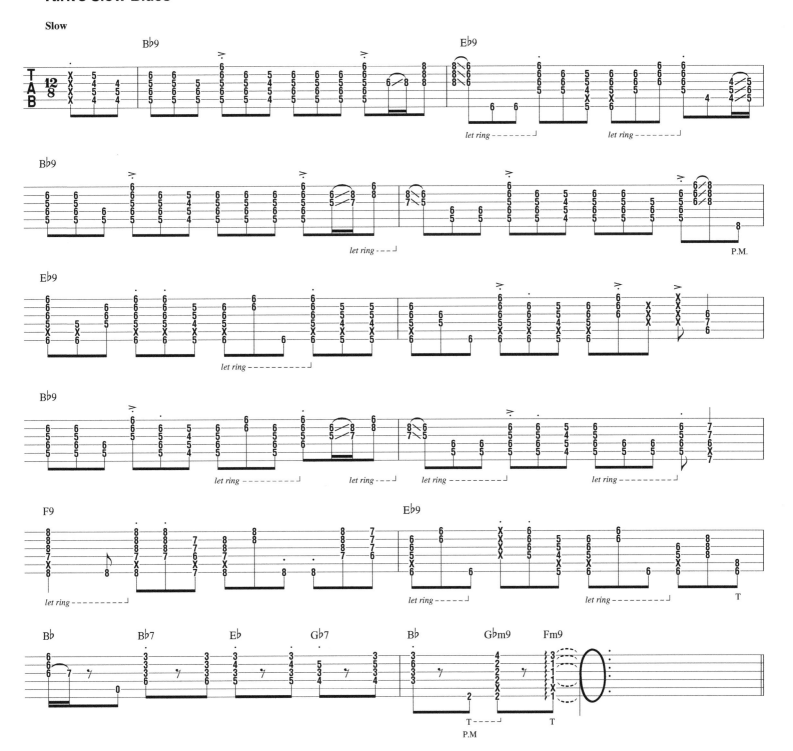

SOLO CONSTRUCTION

Introduction

Blues Scale

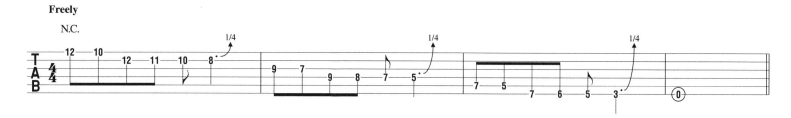

Blues Scale Phrase 1

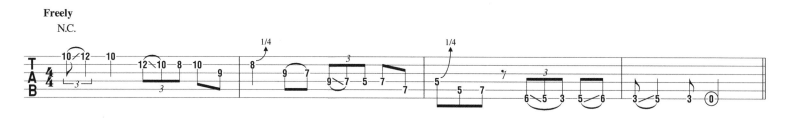

Blues Scale Phrase 2

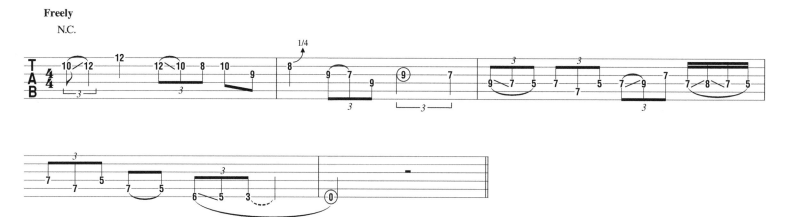

Blues Scale Phrase 3

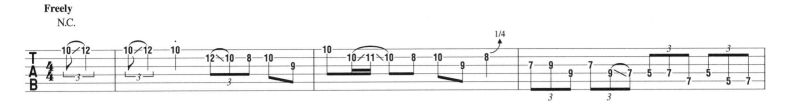

Blues Scale Phrase 4

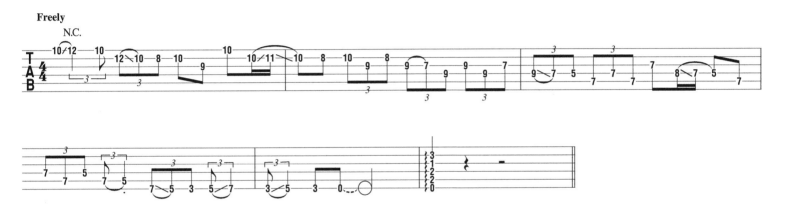

Blues Scale Breakdown

Blues Scale Breakdown w/ bends

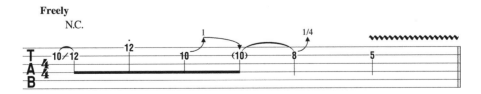

Blues Scale Breakdown w/ licks

Texas Blues

Opening Phrase

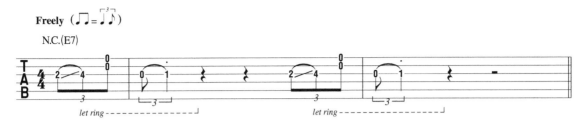

Doublestop Phrase 1

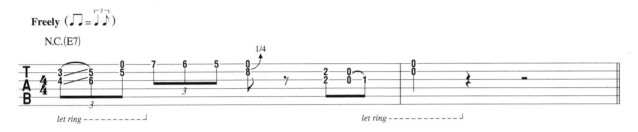

Back Rake Phrase

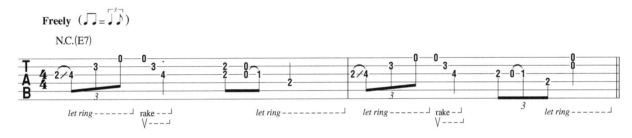

Low String Phrase

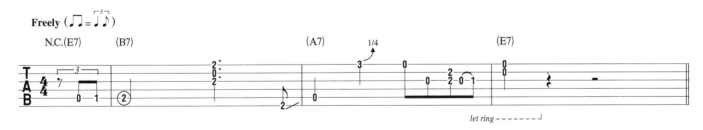

Doublestop Phrase 2

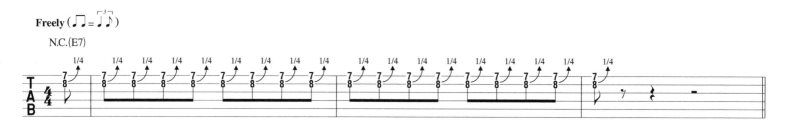

Doublestop Phrase 2A

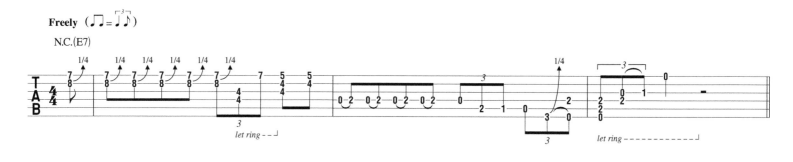

IV Chord Phrase

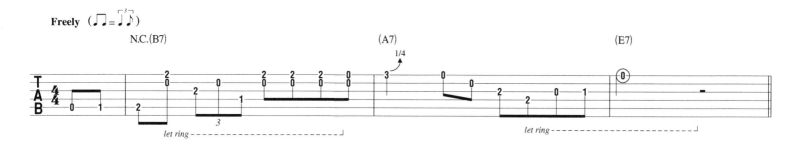

All Together

Moderately

Chicago Blues

Opening Phrase

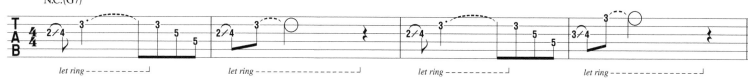

Pedal Point Phrase

Turnaround Phrase

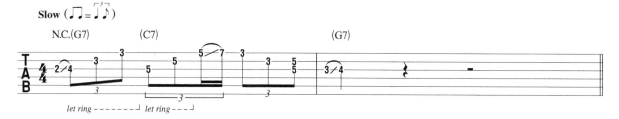

Chord Licks

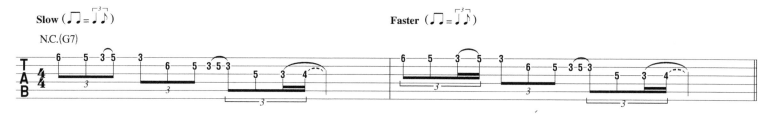

Sliding 6ths

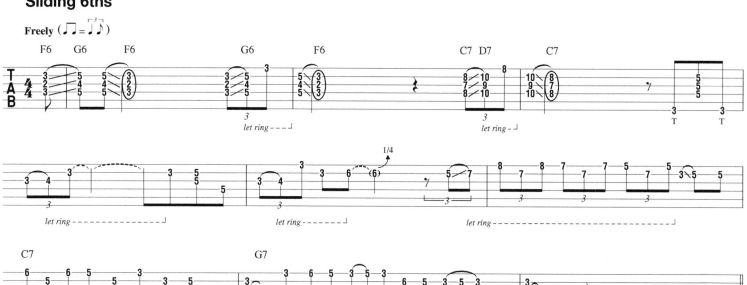

All Together

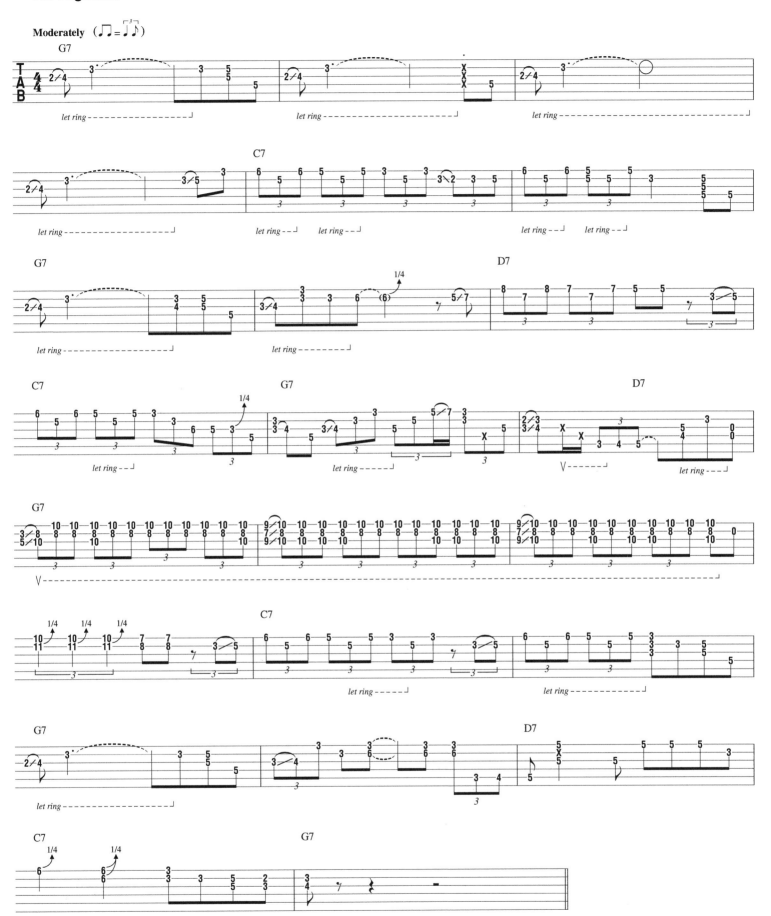

West Coast Jump

Jump Blues Lick 1

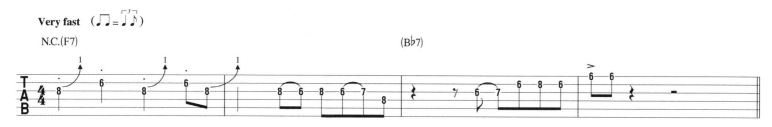

Jump Blues Lick 2

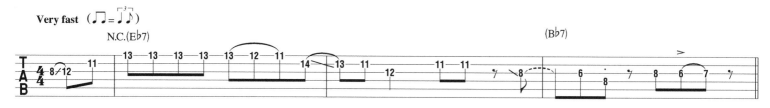

Doublestop Stabs

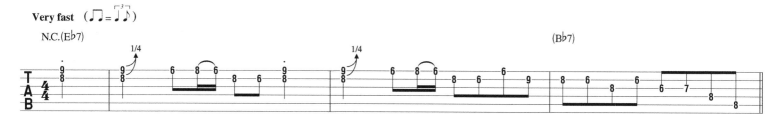

Chromatic Phrasing

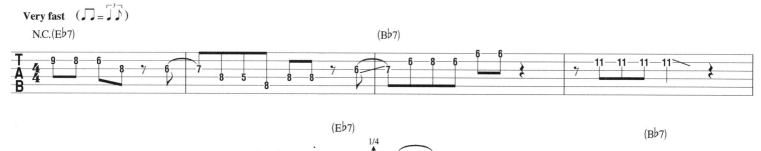

All Together

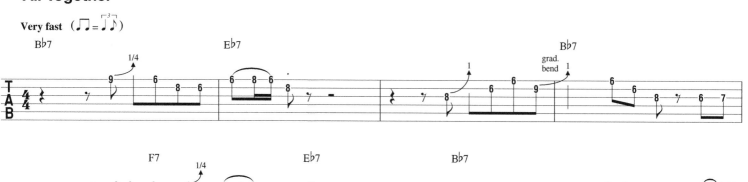

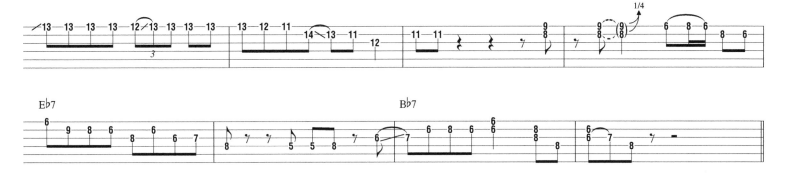

Jump Blues Improv

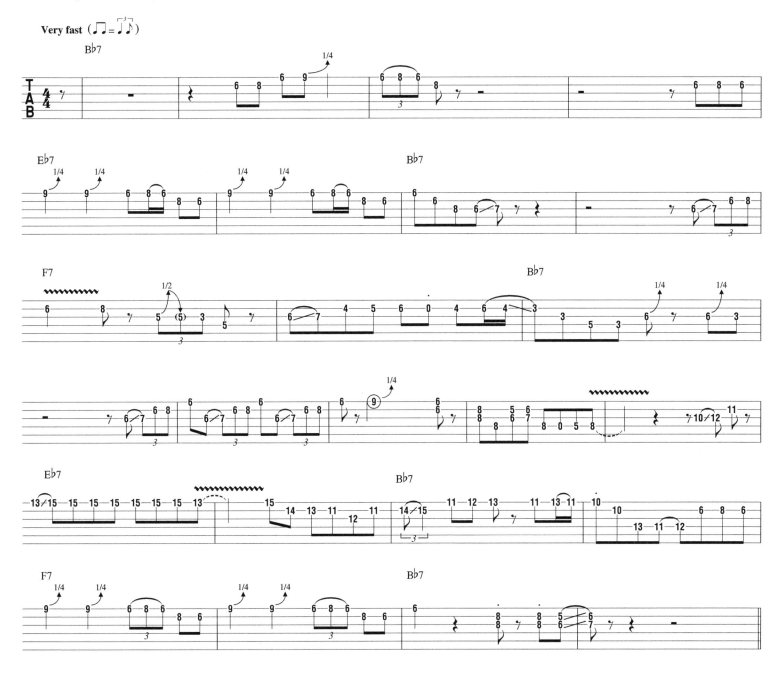

Funky Blues

Funky Blues Phrase 1

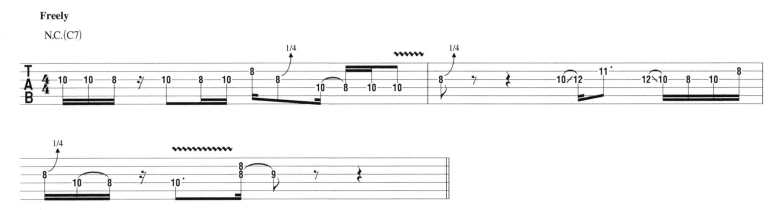

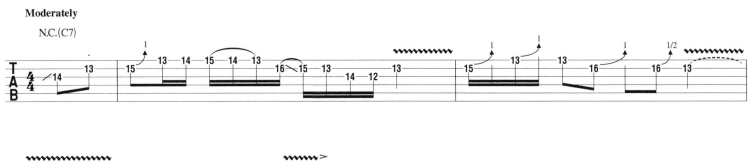

Funky Blues Phrase 2

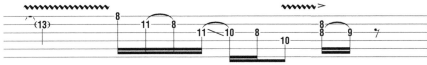

Funky Blues Phrase 3

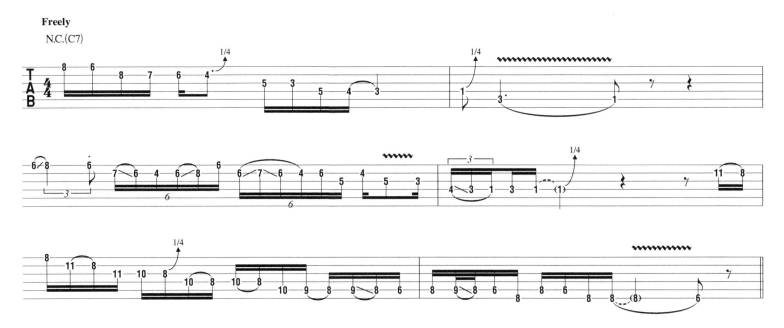

Sequencing

Freely

N.C.(C7)

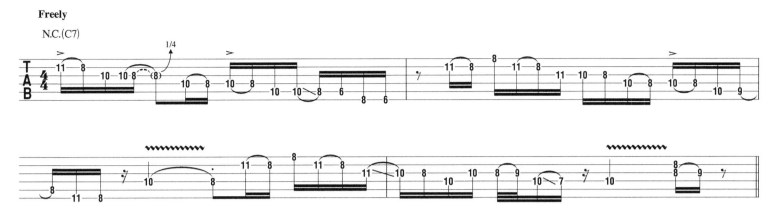

Sliding

Moderately slow

N.C.

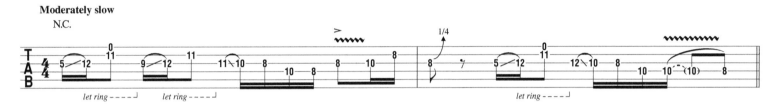

Using Space

Moderately

N.C.(C7)

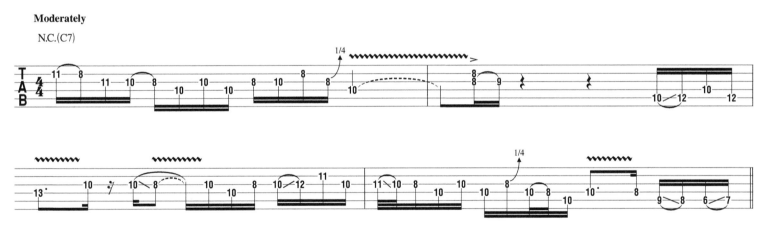

All Together

Moderately

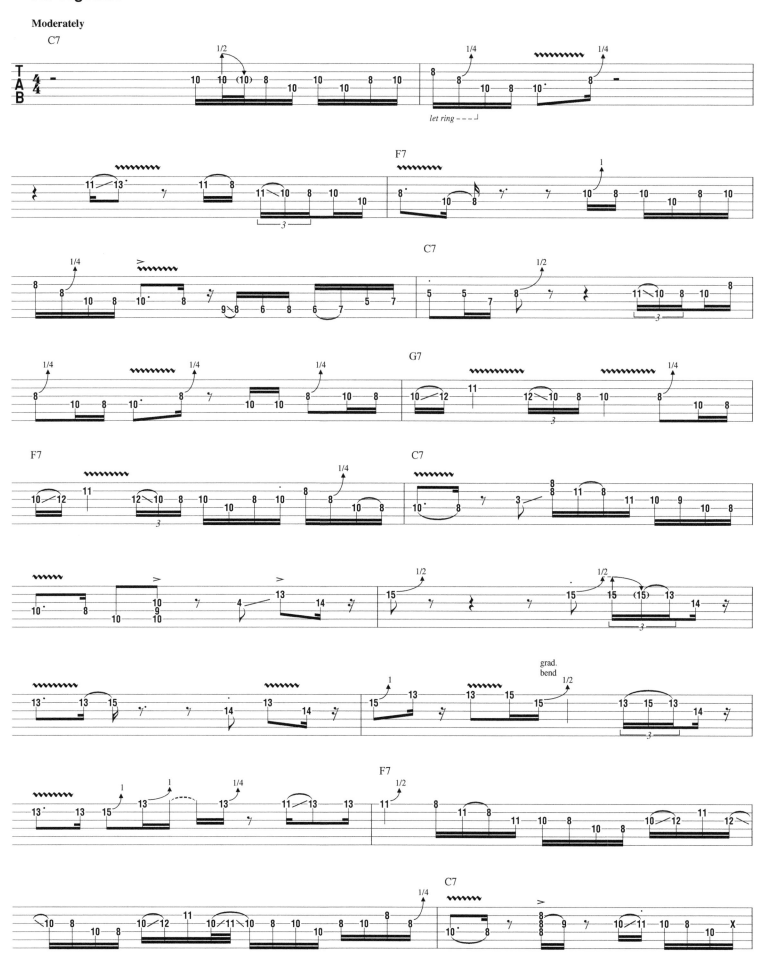

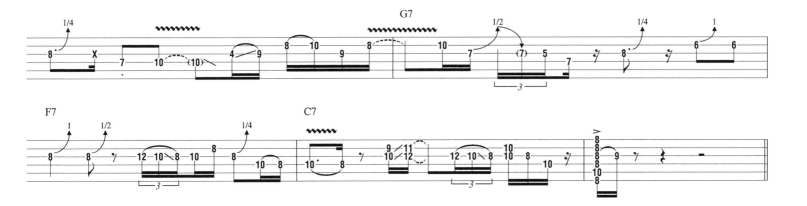

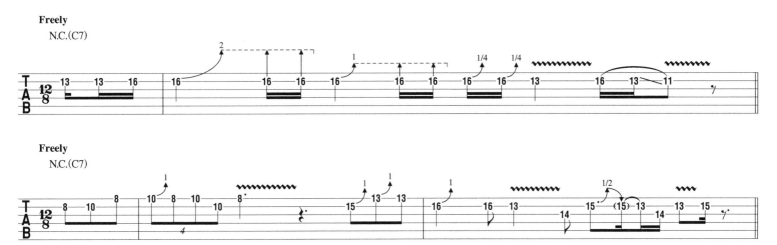

Slow Blues

Albert King Licks

Call and Response

Slow Blues Improv

*Played slightly behind the beat.

Final Solo

*Played ahead of beat.

**Played as even sixteenth notes.

**Played as even sixteenth notes.

***Played as even eighth & sixteenth notes.

RHYTHM TAB LEGEND

Rhythm Tab is a form of notation that adds rhythmic values to the traditional tab staff.

TABLATURE graphically represents the guitar fingerboard. Each horizontal line represents a string, and each number represents a fret. Rhythmic values are shown using ovals, stems, and dots.

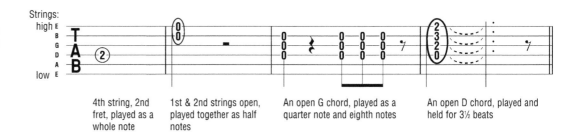

Strings:
high E
B
G
D
A
low E

4th string, 2nd fret, played as a whole note

1st & 2nd strings open, played together as half notes

An open G chord, played as a quarter note and eighth notes

An open D chord, played and held for 3½ beats

Definitions for Special Guitar Notation

HALF-STEP BEND: Strike the note and bend up 1/2 step.

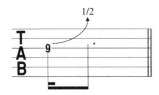

WHOLE-STEP BEND: Strike the note and bend up one step.

GRACE NOTE BEND: Strike the note and immediately bend up as indicated.

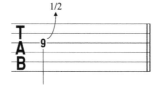

SLIGHT (MICROTONE) BEND: Strike the note and bend up 1/4 step.

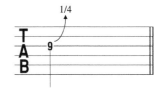

BEND AND RELEASE: Strike the note and bend up as indicated, then release back to the original note. Only the first note is struck.

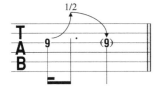

PRE-BEND: Bend the note as indicated, then strike it.

PRE-BEND AND RELEASE: Bend the note as indicated. Strike it and release the bend back to the original note.

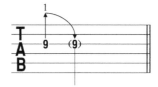

UNISON BEND: Strike the two notes simultaneously and bend the lower note up to the pitch of the higher.

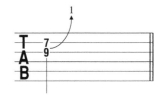

HOLD BEND: While sustaining bent note, strike note on different string.

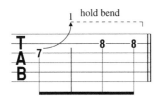

VIBRATO: The string is vibrated by rapidly bending and releasing the note with the fretting hand.

WIDE VIBRATO: The pitch is varied to a greater degree by vibrating with the fretting hand.

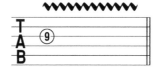

HAMMER-ON: Strike the first (lower) note with one finger, then sound the higher note (on the same string) with another finger by fretting it without picking.

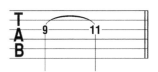

PULL-OFF: Place both fingers on the notes to be sounded. Strike the first note and without picking, pull the finger off to sound the second (lower) note.

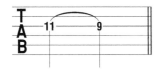

HAMMER FROM NOWHERE: Sound note(s) by hammering with fret hand finger only.

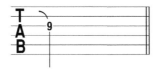

GRACE NOTE SLUR: Strike the note and immediately hammer-on (or pull-off) as indicated.

GRACE NOTE SLUR (CLUSTER): Strike the notes and immediately hammer-on (or pull-off) as indicated.

LEGATO SLIDE: Strike the first note and then slide the same fret-hand finger up or down to the second note. The second note is not struck.

SHIFT SLIDE: Same as legato slide, except the second note is struck.

TRILL: Very rapidly alternate between the notes indicated by continuously hammering on and pulling off.

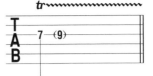

TAPPING: Hammer ("tap") the fret indicated with the pick-hand index or middle finger and pull off to the note fretted by the fret hand.

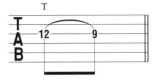

NATURAL HARMONIC: Strike the note while the fret-hand lightly touches the string directly over the fret indicated.

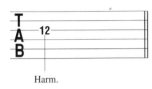

Harm.

PINCH HARMONIC: The note is fretted normally and a harmonic is produced by adding the edge of the thumb or the tip of the index finger of the pick hand to the normal pick attack.

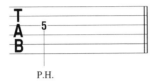

P.H.

HARP HARMONIC: The note is fretted normally and a harmonic is produced by gently resting the pick hand's index finger directly above the indicated fret (in parentheses) while the pick hand's thumb or pick assists by plucking the appropriate string.

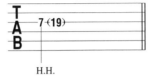

H.H.

PICK SCRAPE: The edge of the pick is rubbed down (or up) the string, producing a scratchy sound.

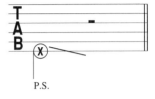

P.S.

MUFFLED STRINGS: A percussive sound is produced by laying the fret hand across the string(s) without depressing, and striking them with the pick hand.

PALM MUTING: The note is partially muted by the pick hand lightly touching the string(s) just before the bridge.

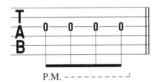

P.M. --------

RAKE: Drag the pick across the strings indicated with a single motion.

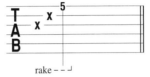

rake - - ⌐

TREMOLO PICKING: The note is picked as rapidly and continuously as possible.

ARPEGGIATE: Play the notes of the chord indicated by quickly rolling them from bottom to top.

VIBRATO BAR DIVE AND RETURN: The pitch of the note or chord is dropped a specified number of steps (in rhythm), then returned to the original pitch.

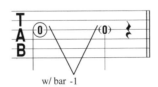

w/ bar -1

VIBRATO BAR SCOOP: Depress the bar just before striking the note, then quickly release the bar.

w/ bar - - - - - - - ⌐

VIBRATO BAR DIP: Strike the note and then immediately drop a specified number of steps, then release back to the original pitch.

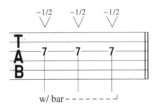

w/ bar - - - - - - ⌐

Additional Musical Definitions

(accent) • Accentuate note (play it louder)

(staccato) • Play the note short

(fermata) • A hold or pause

• Downstroke

V • Upstroke

• Repeat measures between signs

NOTE: Tablature numbers in parentheses are used when:
• The note is sustained, but a new articulation begins (such as a hammer-on, pull-off, slide, or bend), or
• A bend is released.